The Haymarket Square Tragedy

by Michael Burgan

Content Consultant: Leslie Orear,
President,
Illinois Labor History Society

Reading Adviser: Rosemary G. Palmer, Ph.D.,
Department of Literacy, College of Education,
Boise State University

COMPASS POINT

MINNEAPOLIS, MINN

Compass Point Books
3109 West 50th Street, #115
Minneapolis, MN 55410

Visit Compass Point Books on the Internet at *www.compasspointbooks.com*
or e-mail your request to *custserv@compasspointbooks.com*

On the cover: Confrontation between the labor protesters and the police
at Haymarket Square in Chicago, May 4, 1886

Photographs ©: Stock Montage, cover, 29; Prints Old & Rare, back cover (far left); Library of
Congress, back cover, 27, 31; North Wind Picture Archives, 4, 7, 11, 13, 36; Chicago Historical
Society, 5, 9, 15, 19, 22, 24, 25, 26, 30, 32, 33, 38, 40; The Granger Collection, New York, 10, 14,
18, 35; Archivo Iconografico, S.A./Corbis, 16; Mary Evans Picture Library, 20, 23, 34;
Rischitz/Getty Images, 37; Bettmann/Corbis, 39; Tim Boyle/Getty Images, 41.

Editor: Julie Gassman
Designer/Page Production: Bradfordesign, Inc./Bobbie Nuytten
Photo Researcher: Svetlana Zhurkin
Cartographer: XNR Productions, Inc.
Educational Consultant: Diane Smolinski
Library Consultant: Kathleen Baxter

Managing Editor: Catherine Neitge
Creative Director: Keith Griffin
Editorial Director: Carol Jones

Library of Congress Cataloging-in-Publication Data
Burgan, Michael.
  The Haymarket Square tragedy / by Michael Burgan.
     p. cm.—(We the people)
  Includes bibliographical references and index.
  ISBN 0-7565-1265-4 (hardcover)
  ISBN 0-7565-1728-1 (paperback)
  1. Haymarket Square Riot, Chicago, Ill., 1886—Juvenile literature. I. Title. II. We the people
(Series) (Compass Point Books)
  HX846.C4B87 2006
  977.3'11041—dc22   2005002463

TABLE OF CONTENTS

VIOLENCE IN THE STREETS

On May 1, 1886, workers from all over the United States refused to go to work. They were unhappy about the long hours they were forced to work for little pay. They wanted their workday shortened to eight hours. Together, by refusing to work, the strikers had power. In Chicago, railroads, stockyards, and other businesses were forced to close because so many workers went on strike.

Workers striking for an eight-hour workday in New York City

4

During their protest, the workers attended rallies. One such rally was held in front of a factory in Chicago, Illinois, on May 3, 1886. Several thousand men gathered to listen to speeches about workers' rights.

The rally was peaceful to start. But part of the crowd became angry when they noticed some replacement workers coming out of work at McCormick Reaper Works, a nearby factory. The replacement workers had taken jobs at the factory after workers there went on strike in February. The

Riot at McCormick Reaper Works on May 3, 1886

strikers began to yell at the replacement workers and tried to push them back into the factory. A fight broke out, and the police soon arrived. In the violence that followed, police killed at least two strikers and seriously wounded several others.

Some of the leaders who spoke that day believed in anarchism, the idea that people could live peacefully without a government. These anarchists thought that citizens could work together to solve their problems. Many anarchists also supported socialism, a system where all property is owned by society as a whole.

These sorts of views were not popular with many Americans, including the police. Because of this, the anarchists believed that striking workers needed to prepare for future violence with police. They warned workers about this violence in speeches, newspapers, and posters.

Several anarchist leaders decided to meet at Chicago's Haymarket Square the next day to protest the events of May 3. The crowd at Haymarket Square was much smaller than the day before. Anarchist leaders August Spies,

6

Albert Parsons, and Samuel Fielden addressed the crowd of about 200 men. Everything was peaceful—until the very end.

Around 10:15 P.M., about 180 Chicago police officers entered the street and ordered the crowd to go home. Suddenly, a bomb exploded, killing one officer. The police

The crowd grew agitated when the police told them to go home.

began to fire their guns in all directions—even toward each other. When the shooting stopped, six more officers were dead and dozens were wounded. An unknown number of people in the crowd also were killed and wounded. Chicago police arrested eight anarchists, including Spies, Parsons, and Fielden, and charged them with conspiracy in the murder of the officers.

In court, the state of Illinois could not prove that the eight men had anything to do with the bombing. But the state's lawyer argued that the anarchists had called for violence before. Their words had led someone else to take action. In the end, all eight anarchists were found guilty. Seven received death sentences, while the eighth was sentenced to 15 years in prison.

The Haymarket Square tragedy came at a time when many American workers faced difficult conditions. Most business owners resisted workers' efforts to improve their situation. Strikes and violence were common at the time. Many Americans disliked the violence. They also

Albert Parsons

Samuel Fielden

Louis Lingg

August Spies

Michael Schwab

George Engel

Adolph Fischer

Portraits of the seven anarchists who were sentenced to death

feared the socialists and their goals. Most Americans

believed every person had a right to own property or start

a business. Socialism would have denied those rights.

Anarchists and Bomb Throwers

ONE HUNDRED AND TWENTY-EIGHT PAGES.

SIXTEEN PAGES ILLUSTRATIONS.

The Greatest Murder Trial on Record, with Speeches in Full of the Attorneys for the Prosecution and Defense. Profusely Illustrated. Price 25 Cents. Agents Wanted.

G. S. BALDWIN, PUBLISHER, 199 CLARK STREET, CHICAGO.

Art Young later regretted drawing this book cover that supported the trial outcome.

The Haymarket case deeply divided the United States. Some people thought the anarchists did not get a fair trial. Others believed that the anarchists' radical beliefs were a good enough reason to find them guilty. Today, most historians believe that the anarchists' legal rights were denied. Because of their fear of anarchists, Illinois government and business leaders ignored the law that gives all Americans the right to free speech and the right to gather peacefully.

10

THE RISE OF UNIONS

The 19th century brought tremendous changes to the United States. Over the course of 100 years, the nation's population grew from 5.3 million to almost 76 million people, and the number of states nearly tripled. Although almost all Americans lived and worked on farms in 1800, by 1900, millions of people worked in various industries.

The Duquesne factories in Pittsburgh, Pennsylvania, produced steel.

The most important industries included railroads, steel, coal, and textiles. The time period in which the growth of industries and their importance to society took place is called the Industrial Revolution.

Industries grew as people invested money in new factories. The money invested was called capital, and the investors themselves were called capitalists. As a group, the people who worked in the factories were called labor.

In an effort to make money, some capitalists did not treat their workers well. They forced them to work long hours in unsafe factories. They hired children and paid them low wages.

Workers within some industries began to form groups called labor unions. The unions worked to improve conditions and wages for workers. Union members believed they would have more power if they worked together when dealing with capitalists.

The unions' biggest weapon was the strike. Workers would walk off their jobs and refuse to work

Children as young as 5 years old worked in factories.

until the factory owners met their demands. With the workers on strike, factory owners lost money.

Some owners made deals with their workers to end strikes. But others brought in replacement workers, or scabs, as the workers called them. These replacement workers were often immigrants desperate for work.

13

Strikers threaten replacement workers at a New York City construction site.

Replacement workers agreed to work for lower pay than union workers, just to have a job. They risked being attacked. Union workers were angry at these scabs for taking over their jobs.

14

SOCIALISTS, ANARCHISTS, AND UNIONS

By 1886, many different labor unions existed in the United States. The largest was the Knights of Labor. Founded in 1869, the Knights welcomed workers from any industry. In 1878, the union said its goal was "to secure to the toilers a proper share of the wealth they create."

The Knights of Labor wanted to halt child labor, give men and women equal pay for equal work, and limit the workday to eight hours. At the time, most laborers worked 10 to 12

The preamble outlined the Knights of Labor's goals and beliefs.

15

hours a day, six days a week. A typical worker earned less than $3 per day. Today, that would be equal to about $55 a day.

The Knights of Labor did not believe in socialism. They did not think property should be shared equally among all members of a society. However, many other U.S. unions were started by socialist workers. Some were European immigrants. They followed the ideas of two German philosophers, Karl Marx and Friedrich Engels. Marx and Engels believed that workers would one day rebel against capitalists to win true equality and freedom. Socialists believed poor working conditions would

16   *Karl Marx*

come to an end when the workers controlled the factories and the government owned all the industries.

In the United States, socialist labor unions often had different goals. Some wanted to get involved in politics and elect socialists to government. Others believed workers should build stronger unions and force capitalists to improve working conditions.

A small number of socialists believed workers had to arm themselves and be ready to defend their rights against the capitalists. In the future, workers might have to actively fight the capitalists and the police who protected them. These radical socialists were usually labeled anarchists, even if they did not follow all anarchist beliefs.

The use of violence seemed more likely after railroad workers went on strike in 1877. Workers from other industries joined the strike to show their support. In many cities, including Chicago, police and Army troops fired on disorderly crowds of strikers. At times, innocent people watching the protests were also killed.

On July 20, 1877, 12 people were killed in Baltimore, Maryland, when Army troops fired into a crowd of strikers during the "Great Uprising."

During this "Great Uprising of 1877," union workers in Chicago were not allowed to hold meetings. Albert Parsons lived in Chicago at the time. He described what he saw in 1877 when police raided a union meeting: "The police broke down the doors … and clubbed and fired upon the men as they struggled … to escape from the building, killing one workman and wounding many others."

STRIKING FOR THE EIGHT-HOUR DAY

Anarchists, socialists, and other labor union leaders often disagreed with each other. But by 1886, they all agreed on wanting to limit the workday to eight hours. Union workers across the country agreed to go on strike on May 1 and demand an eight-hour day. Because of its many factories and labor unions, Chicago was at the center of the eight-hour day movement.

Albert Parsons was one of the leading anarchists in Chicago. He often worked with August Spies, another leading anarchist. Together,

Albert Parsons

19

they wrote important anarchist documents and spoke to workers across the Midwest. Parsons was also editor of a newspaper called *The Alarm*. Its articles sometimes talked about the violence that could occur as workers fought for control of society. The paper's writers often wrote about using dynamite as a weapon. Anarchists thought that if they had dynamite bombs, the police would be less likely to attack them.

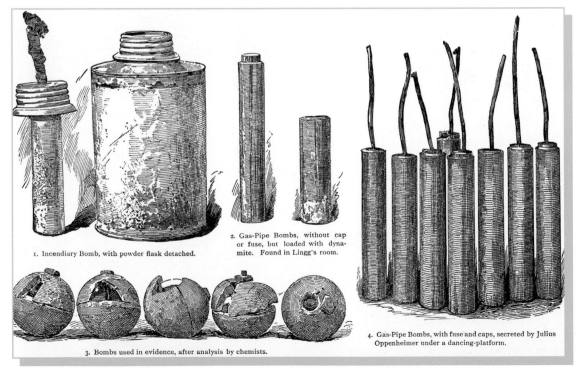

1. Incendiary Bomb, with powder flask detached.

2. Gas-Pipe Bombs, without cap or fuse, but loaded with dynamite. Found in Lingg's room.

3. Bombs used in evidence, after analysis by chemists.

4. Gas-Pipe Bombs, with fuse and caps, secreted by Julius Oppenheimer under a dancing-platform.

This illustration of bombs made by anarchists appeared in a book published in 1889.

On May 1, 1886, tens of thousands of Chicago workers went on strike to support the eight-hour workday. Local newspapers warned that if violence occurred, Parsons and Spies would probably be to blame. But the protests that day were peaceful. On May 3, however, trouble erupted.

On the first day of the eight-hour workday strike, 80,000 workers marched down Michigan Avenue, an important street in Chicago.

21

That afternoon, Spies spoke to a crowd of about 5,000 striking men. The audience included workers from McCormick Reaper Works, a factory that made farm equipment. Union members there had gone on strike in February, and the factory's owners had brought in replacement workers.

August Spies

Some of the McCormick workers left Spies' speech to yell at the scabs as they left the nearby factory. Others in the crowd joined them. The striking union workers tried to force the replacement workers back into the factory. As the shoving and

22

yelling went on, about 200 police officers reached the scene. They began firing into the crowd to try to gain control of the fighting.

August Spies later recalled how he felt as he watched the police shoot the workers. "My blood was boiling, and I think in that moment I could have done almost anything, seeing men, women, and children fired upon, people who

An 1886 newspaper illustration of police firing into the crowds at McCormick Reaper Works

23

REVENGE!

Workingmen, to Arms!!!

Your masters sent out their bloodhounds—the police—; they killed six of your brothers at McCormicks this afternoon. They killed the poor wretches, because they, like you, had the courage to disobey the supreme will of your bosses. They killed them, because they dared ask for the shortening of the hours of toil. They killed them to show you, "Free American Citizens!" that you must be satisfied and contended with whatever your bosses condescend to allow you, or you will get killed!

You have for years endured the most abject humiliations; you have for years suffered unmeasurable iniquities; you have worked yourself to death; you have endured the pangs of want and hunger; your Children you have sacrificed to the factory-lords—in short: You have been miserable and obedient slave all these years: Why? To satisfy the insatiable greed, to fill the coffers of your lazy thieving master? When you ask them now to lessen your burden, he sends his bloodhounds out to shoot you, kill you!

If you are men, if you are the sons of your grand sires, who have shed their blood to free you, then you will rise in your might, Hercules, and destroy the hideous monster that seeks to destroy you. To arms we call you, to arms!

Your Brothers.

Rache! Rache!

Arbeiter, zu den Waffen!

Arbeitendes Volk, heute Nachmittag mordeten die Bluthunde Eurer Ausbeuter 6 Eurer Brüder draußen bei McCormick's. Warum mordeten sie dieselben? Weil sie den Muth hatten, mit dem Loos unzufrieden zu sein, welches Eure Ausbeuter ihnen beschieden haben. Sie forderten Brod, man antwortete ihnen mit Blei, eingedenk der Thatsache, daß man damit das Volk am wirksamsten zum Schweigen bringen kann! Viele, viele Jahre habt Ihr alle Demüthigungen ohne Widerspruch ertragen, habt Euch vom frühen Morgen bis zum späten Abend geschunden, habt Entbehrungen jeder Art ertragen, habt Eure Kinder selbst geopfert—Alles, um die Schatzkammern Eurer Herren zu füllen, Alles für sie! Und jetzt, wo Ihr vor sie hintretet, und sie ersucht, Eure Bürde etwas zu erleichtern, da hetzen sie zum Dank für Eure Opfer ihre Bluthunde, die Polizei, auf Euch, um Euch mit Bleikugeln von der Unzufriedenheit zu kuriren Sklaven, wir tragen und beschwören Euch bei Allem, was Euch heilig und werth ist, rächt diesen schändlichen Mord, den man heute an Euren Brüdern beging, und vielleicht morgen schon an Euch begehen wird. Arbeitendes Volk, Herkules, Du bist am Scheideweg angelangt. Wofür entscheidest Du Dich? Für Sklaverei und Hunger, oder für Freiheit und Brod? Entscheidest Du Dich für das Letztere, dann säume keinen Augenblick; dann, Volk, zu den Waffen! Vernichtung den menschlichen Bestien, die sich Deine Herrscher nennen! Rücksichtslose Vernichtung ihnen—das muß Deine Losung sein! Denk' der Helden, deren Blut den Weg zum Fortschritt, zur Freiheit und zur Menschlichkeit gedüngt—und strebe, ihrer würdig zu werden!

Eure Brüder.

Albert Spies' "Workingmen to Arms!!!" poster

were not armed fired upon by policemen."

In his anger, Spies wrote a poster in both English and German. A printer added the word "Revenge!" at the top. Spies titled it "Workingmen, To Arms!!!" and began, "Your masters sent out their bloodhounds—the police—; they killed six of your brothers this afternoon." Spies challenged his readers to fight to defend their rights.

24

PROTESTING POLICE VIOLENCE

On the night of May 3, a group of anarchists met to discuss what happened at the McCormick factory. They included George Engel and Adolph Fischer, two anarchists who were willing to go to extreme lengths for their beliefs. The anarchists decided to hold a rally the next day at Haymarket Square to protest the violence. Fischer took charge of printing posters for the rally. He promised "good speakers" would be there.

Adolph Fischer

The next day, Fischer asked Spies to speak. Spies agreed to speak if Fischer took out a line in the poster that

25

told working men "to arm yourselves and appear in full force." The poster was changed, but a few of the original posters were handed out.

Spies arrived at Haymarket Square a little after 8 o'clock that night. He was disappointed to see just a few thousand people there. He had hoped the rally would draw 25,000 people. The people who were there were beginning to leave, since no speakers had arrived. Spies quickly jumped onto a wagon parked just off the square. Before addressing the crowd, Spies sent a friend to find Albert Parsons and Samuel Fielden, so they could also speak at the rally.

A few thousand people gathered at Haymarket Square.

After Spies finished his speech, Parsons spoke for about an hour. He talked about the violence the day before at the McCormick factory, but he did not call for the workers to fight back with their own weapons.

Chicago's government leaders knew about the Haymarket rally, and they feared violence could break out. Mayor Carter Harrison joined the crowd that gathered that night. He wanted to hear for himself what the anarchists would say. Police detectives in plain clothes passed on reports of what they saw and heard to police inspector John Bonfield. The inspector had extra officers nearby if any trouble began.

Carter Harrison

Harrison left the rally just before Parsons finished speaking. He stopped to see Bonfield. As the mayor later said, he told Bonfield, "Nothing had occurred yet, or looked likely to occur to require interference." The mayor then suggested that Bonfield send the extra officers home, and the inspector agreed. But instead, just a few minutes later, Bonfield and Captain William Ward led about 180 officers to Haymarket Square.

As the police arrived, Samuel Fielden was just ending his speech. Ward told the crowd to leave the area. Fielden replied, "Why, captain, this is a peaceable meeting." Ward repeated his order. Spies and Fielden jumped off the wagon and headed for the sidewalk.

Suddenly, an explosion shook the crowd, and almost immediately the police began to fire. Fielden later wrote, "I saw a flash in the middle of the street and heard the explosion of the bomb. … The crowd ran in every direction. Immediately after the explosion,

The bomb at Haymarket killed one police officer and injured several other people.

I was struck in the knee by a bullet. … I felt the blow, but did not know what it was."

The workers ducked as police fired their guns and swung their clubs. Others tried to run. Some officers were

29

This illustration of Desplaines Street Police Station following the violence appeared in The Graphic News *on May 15, 1886.*

struck by bullets from other police officers. Within a few minutes, the violence ended. The police carried the wounded and dead officers back to the station. The workers and speakers went home or looked for doctors to treat their wounds.

THE TRIAL

The Chicago police began to hunt down known anarchists and socialists in the city. They wanted to arrest the bomb thrower and anyone else who might have been involved. On May 5, Mayor Harrison released a statement. He blamed the tragedy on "a body of lawless men," meaning the anarchists and socialists. These people, he said, claimed they wanted to help labor, but in reality, they wanted

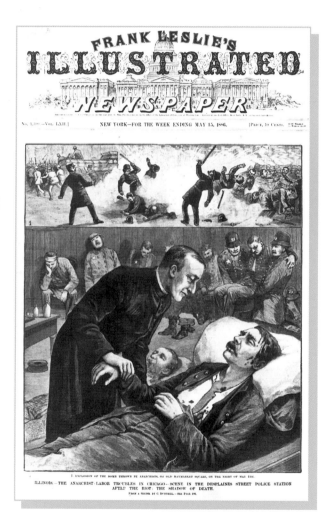

Many newspapers sympathized with the police.

31

The trial took place at the Cook County Criminal Court Building.

"to destroy all law." Harrison gave the police the power to break up any meetings that threatened law and order.

By the end of May, the police had accused 31 people of conspiracy. They were also charged with helping to murder the police officer killed when the bomb exploded. Eight men went on trial, including Spies, Parsons, Fielden, Engel, and Fischer. The others were Michael Schwab, Louis Lingg, and Oscar Neebe.

All of the men except Parsons and Neebe had been born in Europe, and Neebe had spent much of his life in

Germany. To many Americans, the men fit the common image of anarchists. They were immigrants who brought strange and dangerous ideas with them to the United States.

Many newspapers, ministers, and public officials spoke out against the accused anarchists. One St. Louis newspaper wrote, "There are no good anarchists except dead anarchists." Most Americans opposed the radical changes that anarchists and socialists wanted to make. They wanted a democratic government and the right to own private property. Most Americans respected police officers and the work they did. They were angry that anarchists would try to attack officers.

Prosecutor Julius Grinnell worked as the state's lawyer at the trial. His job was to prove that the eight anarchists

Julius Grinnell

were guilty. He did not claim that any of the men threw the bomb. No one knew who had thrown it. But the anarchists, Grinnell said, "are as responsible as the actual thrower."

Grinnell showed that the anarchists had often spoken and written about changing the United States through violence. Their words had influenced the bomb thrower to carry out the attack. Grinnell told the jury to "make examples of [the eight men], hang them and you save our institutions, our society." He used Americans' fear of anarchy and violence to stir hatred for the accused men.

34

An 1887 illustration by William Ottman of the trial of the eight accused anarchists

The lawyers defending the eight anarchists attacked Grinnell and his witnesses for lying. They offered proof that some of the accused men were not even near Haymarket Square on May 4. None of the men had called for violence that night. The lawyers also looked to the U.S. Constitution. It gives everyone the right to speak freely and meet with others to discuss their ideas. The accused men had the right to hold labor meetings and write about anarchy and violence.

On August 20, the jury found all eight men guilty. Each of the anarchists then had a chance to address the court. Spies said the only crime the men committed was "that they dared to speak the truth." Michael Schwab said the trial was "directed against the labor movement," since none of the eight had been involved in the bombing.

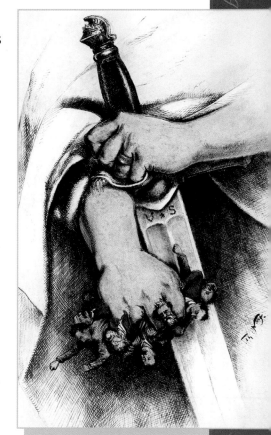

An 1886 cartoon by Thomas Nast celebrated the guilty verdict.

35

PRISON AND DEATH

All of the anarchists except Neebe were sentenced to die. Neebe received a 15-year prison sentence. After the trial, their lawyers filed an appeal. With an appeal, another court considers the facts of a legal case and looks for any errors in the first trial. The eight anarchists appealed their case to the most powerful court in the state, the Illinois Supreme Court.

In 1887, that court said the original decision was correct. Later that year, the lawyers asked

August Spies sits in his jail cell.

the most powerful court in the country, the U.S. Supreme Court, to hear the case. The Supreme Court refused to consider the appeal.

36

As the appear process went on, Americans continued to debate the Haymarket trial. Anarchists and socialists defended the eight men. A well-known writer, William Dean Howells, also spoke out for the men. He disliked the anarchists' beliefs, but he

William Dean Howells

thought they had not received a fair trial. The anarchists, Howell wrote, "were doomed to suffer for their opinion's sake." Most people, however, believed the eight men were guilty, even if they did not throw the bomb.

Some of the men who were sentenced to die wrote to Illinois Governor Richard Oglesby from prison. August Spies asked the governor to kill him and let the others go free. Fielden and Schwab asked Oglesby to use his legal power to change their sentences to life in prison. Oglesby agreed, but the death sentences for the five who did not ask for lesser sentences remained. Rather than be hanged, Louis Lingg killed himself in his jail cell. On November 11, 1887, Parsons, Fischer, Engel, and Spies were hanged.

The four men were soon called martyrs. More than 150,000 people filled the streets of Chicago for their funeral. Labor leaders and others kept working to get Neebe, Fielden, and Schwab out of jail.

Thousands joined in the funeral march of the executed anarchists.

Finally in 1893, a new Illinois governor took action. John P. Altgeld was a lawyer and a judge before he was elected governor. He carefully read all the information from the trial.

Altgeld found major problems with how Julius Grinnell and Judge Joseph Gary had carried out the trial. Grinnell had unfairly picked jurors who were likely to believe the anarchists were guilty. The judge, Altgeld said, made a mistake when he said the state did not have to know who the bomb-thrower was or prove he had read the anarchists' newspapers or posters. The governor also said some of the witnesses for the state lied. "It is clearly my duty," the governor wrote, "to act in this case … and … grant an absolute pardon to Samuel Fielden, Oscar Neebe, and Michael Schwab."

John P. Altgeld

Altgeld's pardon freed the three anarchists from jail. The legal battles were over, but the Haymarket tragedy and trial had some lasting effects. Fewer workers were willing to call themselves anarchists and socialists, though many still supported the work of labor unions. People who had radical ideas were sometimes attacked as anarchists, even if they were not. To avoid problems, the largest unions would no longer talk about ending government or private property.

To the police officers of Chicago, the bombing and trial highlighted the difficult work they

A statue honoring the seven police who were killed was erected in 1889. It has been moved several times.

40

The Haymarket Memorial marks the location of the Haymarket Square tragedy.

do. They were glad that Grinnell and Gary were able to convince the jurors that the anarchists were guilty.

For other Americans, the tragedy showed that the U.S. legal system did not always work as it should. The eight anarchists were denied their rights because of what they wrote and spoke. Today, the trial serves as a reminder that the right to speak freely and gather peacefully is valuable and should not be taken for granted.

GLOSSARY

anarchism—a social system that calls for ending government and having people solve their problems as a group without elected leadership

conspiracy—a plot among a group of people to commit a crime

Constitution—the document that describes the basic laws and principles by which the United States is governed

executed—put to death as punishment for a crime

labor unions—organized groups of workers who try to improve working conditions and pay

martyrs—people who give their lives for a worthy cause

radical—extreme or beyond what most people agree with

socialism—an economic system in which the government owns most businesses

strike—when workers refuse to work, hoping to force their employer to agree to their demands

toilers—workers

42

DID YOU KNOW?

- Rudolph Schnaubelt, the brother-in-law of Michael Schwab, was accused of being the bomb-thrower at Haymarket Square. He disappeared before the trial and fled the United States. Witnesses could not say for sure if Schnaubelt threw the bomb. Historians are still not sure who threw it.

- In 1893, a statue honoring the Haymarket martyrs was placed at their cemetery in Forest Park, just outside Chicago. The National Park Service made the statue a National Historic Landmark in 1997. Other important American socialists have chosen to be buried near the executed anarchists.

- Louis Lingg was an expert with dynamite and other explosives. He was accused of making the bomb thrown at Haymarket Square. Lingg killed himself by placing a small explosive device in his mouth.

- After the Haymarket Square trial, U.S. labor leaders convinced European socialists to celebrate May 1 as a special holiday for workers. "May Day" is still celebrated as a labor celebration around the world, although not in the United States.

IMPORTANT DATES

Timeline

1877
During the "Great Uprising of 1877," police kill strikers and innocent bystanders in Chicago and other cities.

1886
On May 1, workers across the United States strike for an eight-hour workday. On May 3, Chicago police fire on strikers at the McCormick Reaper Works. On May 4, anarchists hold a rally near Chicago's Haymarket Square to protest those shootings. A bomb explodes and police open fire. A number of people are killed, including seven police officers. On August 20, eight anarchists are found guilty for causing the violence at Haymarket Square.

1887
Four of the eight anarchists are executed, one kills himself, and the rest remain in prison.

1893
Illinois Governor John P. Altgeld pardons the three surviving anarchists. A memorial statue for the martyrs is placed at their cemetery.

IMPORTANT PEOPLE

JOHN P. ALTGELD (1847–1902)

Governor of Illinois who pardoned three of the anarchists found guilty after the Haymarket Square tragedy

SAMUEL FIELDEN (1847–1922)

One of three anarchists pardoned after the Haymarket Square trial

ADOLPH FISCHER (1858–1887)

One of the leading anarchists in Chicago who was found guilty and executed after the Haymarket Square tragedy

JULIUS GRINNELL (1842–1898)

Prosecutor for the state of Illinois during the trial after the Haymarket Square tragedy

ALBERT PARSONS (1848–1887)

One of the leading anarchists in Chicago who was found guilty and executed after the Haymarket Square tragedy

AUGUST SPIES (1855–1887)

One of the leading anarchists in Chicago who was found guilty and executed after the Haymarket Square tragedy

WANT TO KNOW MORE?

At the Library

Collier, Christopher, and James Collier. *The Rise of Industry, 1860-1900*. New York: Benchmark Books, 2000.

Fireside, Bryna J. *The Haymarket Square Riot Trial*. Berkeley Heights, N.J.: Enslow Publishers, 2002.

Meltzer, Milton. *Bread and Roses: The Struggle of American Labor 1865-1915*. Bridgewater, N.J.: Replica Books, 1999.

On the Web

For more information on *Haymarket Square Tragedy*, use FactHound to track down Web sites related to this book.

1. Go to *www.facthound.com*

2. Type in a search word related to this book or this book ID: 0756512654

3. Click on the *Fetch It* button.

Your trusty FactHound will fetch the best Web sites for you!

On the Road

Forest Home Cemetery

863 S. Des Plaines Ave.

Forest Park, IL 60130

708/366-1900

To see the memorial statue that honors the anarchists executed after the Haymarket Square tragedy

Haymarket Square Memorial

Des Plaines Avenue and

Randolph Street

Chicago, IL 60661

To see the site where the Haymarket Square tragedy took place

Look for more We the People books about this era:

Angel Island

The Great Chicago Fire

*Great Women of the
     Suffrage Movement*

The Harlem Renaissance

The Hindenburg

Industrial America

The Johnstown Flood

The Lowell Mill Girls

Roosevelt's Rough Riders

A complete list of We the People titles is available on our Web site:
www.compasspointbooks.com

INDEX

About the Author

Michael Burgan is a freelance writer of books for children and adults. A history graduate of the University of Connecticut, he has written more than 90 fiction and nonfiction children's books for various publishers. For adult audiences, he has written news articles, essays, and plays. Michael Burgan is a recipient of an Educational Press Association of America award.